spot

CREEPY CRAWLIES

BEETLES

by Nessa Black

AMICUS | AMICUS INK

hard wings

jaws

Look for these
words and pictures
as you read.

legs

soft wings

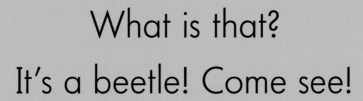

What is that?

It's a beetle! Come see!

There are many kinds of beetles.
All beetles are insects.

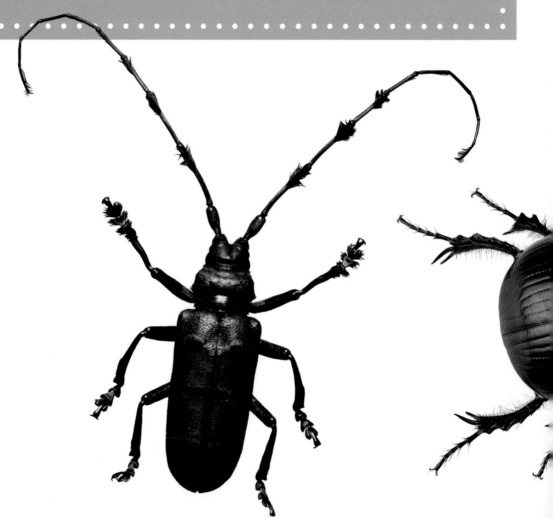

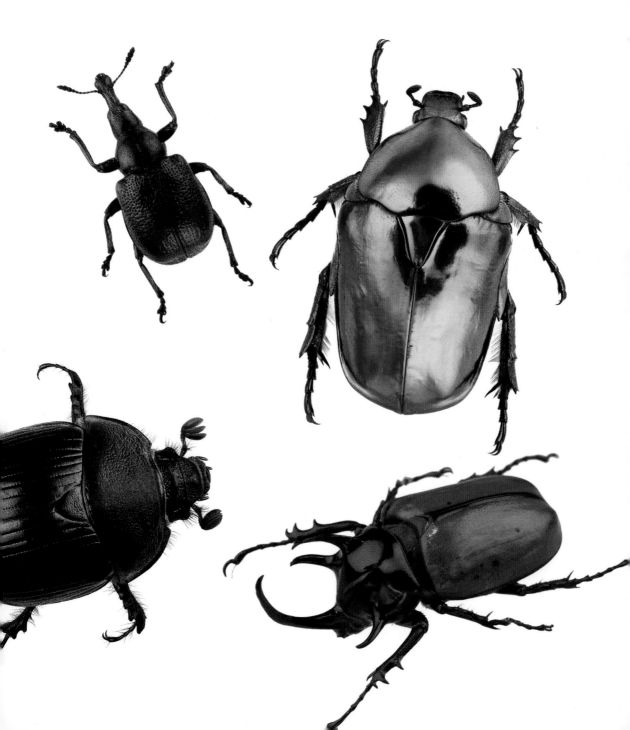

Look at its legs. It has six.
It makes sound by
rubbing its legs.

legs

Look at its jaws.
They hold food.
They fight.

jaws

Look at its hard wings.
They are like a shell.
They protect the soft wings.

hard wings

Look at the soft wings.
They are used to fly.

soft wings

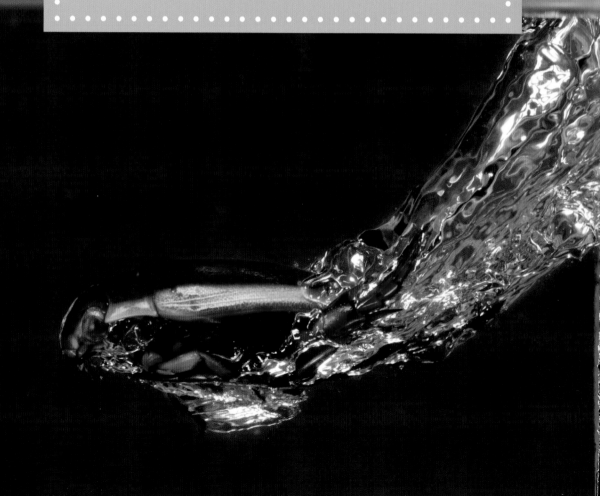

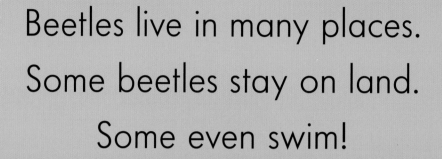

Beetles live in many places.
Some beetles stay on land.
Some even swim!

Look at its hard wings.
They are like a shell.
They protect the soft wings.
hard wings

Look at its jaws.
They hold food.
They fight.
jaws

hard wings

jaws

Did you find?

legs

soft wings

Look at its legs. It has six.
It makes sound by
rubbing its legs.
legs

Look at the soft wings.
They are used to fly.
soft wings

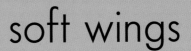

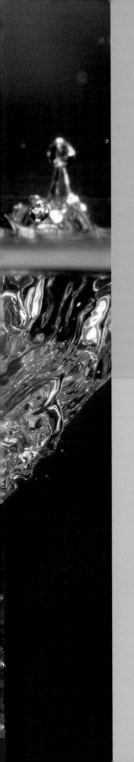

Spot is published by Amicus and Amicus Ink
P.O. Box 1329, Mankato, MN 56002
www.amicuspublishing.us

Library of Congress Cataloging-in-Publication Data
Names: Black, Nessa, author.
Title: Beetles / by Nessa Black.
Description: Mankato, Minnesota : Amicus, [2018] | Series:
   Spot. Creepy crawlies | Audience: K to grade 3.
Identifiers: LCCN 2016055563 (print) | LCCN 2016059926
   (ebook) | ISBN 9781681511061 (library binding) | ISBN
   9781681522258 (pbk.) | ISBN 9781681511962 (e-book)
Subjects: LCSH: Beetles--Juvenile literature.
Classification: LCC QL576.2 .B53 2018 (print) | LCC
   QL576.2 (ebook) | DDC 595.76--dc23
LC record available at https://lccn.loc.gov/2016055563

Printed in China

HC 10 9 8 7 6 5 4 3 2 1
PB 10 9 8 7 6 5 4 3 2 1

Wendy Dieker, editor
Deb Miner, series designer
Ciara Beitlich, book designer
Holly Young, photo researcher

Photos by AgeFotoStock 4;
Alamy 5; Getty cover; iStock 1,
6–7, 8–9, 10–11; Minden Pictures
14–15; Shutterstock 4–5, 12–13;
WikiCommons 3

BEETLES